Would you Respond to "China's Cry" for Bibles?

宋能爾佈道團 敬贈

Together, we can arm underground Christians in China with their most powerful weapon— CHINESE LANGUAGE BIBLES!

The greatest need for underground Christians is Chinese Bibles!

The Battle for the Chinese Bible

by
Nora Lam

with Wm. Thomas Bray

Foreword by Pastor Dennis Balcombe

CHINA TODAY BOOKS
Post Office Box 24466
San Jose, CA 95154 USA

Contents

China Today Books is a division of Nora Lam Chinese Ministries
International, P.O. Box 24466, San Jose, CA 95154.

Copyright © 1997 by Nora Lam Chinese Ministries International.
Front Cover by Janell Robertson.
Front cover photograph: SuperStock, Inc.

Printed in USA

*The dragon went to make
war . . . with those which have
the testimony of Jesus Christ.*
Revelation 12:17

Preface

For centuries, tyrants in the largest nation on earth have tried in vain to suppress one little book. And never more than today. Hard-line Chinese Communist Party fanatics fear the Bible more than ever before — more than any book ever written.

This hatred of God's Word is so intense that human rights are routinely sacrificed to stop Bible distribution.

> • Annually, millions of Chinese tax dollars are spent to destroy it. Monthly, PSB secret police work thousands of hours to hunt down and jail Bible distributors. Every jurisdiction — every state, city, and special administrative region — must maintain and staff whole departments for this cause. Enforcing the ban on the Chinese Bible is an industry!

• Hundreds of thousands of innocent people have been murdered or tortured to prevent the Word of God from reaching the minds of the Chinese people.

• Over 1,100 concentration camps are devoted in part to imprisoning Chinese Bible students. Thousands of jail cells, dungeons, and torture chambers warehouse Chinese Christian prisoners. *Most of these Chinese Christian prisoners are detained on charges related to Bible study.*

Why do China's rulers so fear the Bible in their own language? The book you are about to read gives the answer. It is a rare glimpse into the Red Dragon's bizarre campaign against Christ and the Bible — the greatest attempt at censorship in the history of the human race.

The Battle for the Chinese Bible tells an incredible story. It is the drama of how the world's biggest and fastest-growing superpower is unable to stop the Word of God.

It is a book to read and pass along. You'll want to give copies to your friends, pastors, Christian leaders, congressional representatives — and Chinese neighbors.

Acknowledgments

First of all, we appreciate the dangerous and heroic work of Pastor Danyun. It was Brother Danyun (along with Brother Bray) who traveled thousands of miles in the Peoples Republic of China to document the true stories in this book. Many are adapted with permission from *Lilies Among Thorns*. We are also grateful for the translation work of Chinese co-workers in Hong Kong, Special Administrative Region, China.

Next, I express gratitude to my son, Dr. Joseph Lam. He is fearlessly carrying on the Nora Lam China Bible Project which I began — expanding it into the 21st century. Without his dedication, this book would never have been published. Joseph Lam's staff team worked many hours to finalize this book. We must mention Kay Wheeler, editor, and Jack Sheline, consultant, by name, but many others helped.

Finally, our special appreciation to my co-author, William Thomas Bray. Brother Bray is a missionary journalist who has traveled into China 11 times in the process of assisting with this book.

We must not forget the precious Chinese underground Christians who risk their lives every day in the battle for the Chinese Bible.

Nora Lam

Foreword

by Pastor Dennis Balcombe

Never has a book been published at a more timely moment. We are beginning an exciting new era in Chinese history. China is modernizing. Rearming. Rebuilding. Global experts and futurists predict that the 21st century will be the "Chinese century" — just as the 20th century was known as the "American century."

I have watched Joseph Lam plan for the 21st century along with the Nora Lam Chinese Ministries International team. We appreciate their efforts to help supply over one million Bibles to the Chinese people.

I commend this valuable book. It is a "must read" for every Christian today. I pray that it will have the widest circulation possible throughout the USA — and the world.

The Lams share our heavenly vision for the great future of China. While it appears that the Red Dragon of Revelation 20:2 is in control of China now, we know the Lord Jesus Christ is soon coming to "cast him into the bottomless pit."

We see a clear vision of the Bible ministry extending into Human, Hubei, Anhui, Hebei, Beijing, Manchuria, Shanxi, Shaanxi, Sichuan, and on to Gansu and Xinjian, and into Afghanistan and the Middle East.

Missionaries from China will take the Bible into Iran, Iraq, Syria, and even the republics of the former Soviet Union. In fact, the vision we see is China missionaries crossing the seas to take the Gospel to the whole world.

What a beautiful blueprint. God's love is so wide and deep. He has not forgotten the 1.2 billion Chinese people. And He has not forgotten the 2 billion non-Chinese people in the Asia Pacific Rim nations who live under Chinese cultural and economic influence.

Christ's purposes for China will be fulfilled through His unlimited wisdom and power. He will complete the work He has begun! And I believe that He plans to continue to use Nora Lam Chinese Ministries International to help do it.

So please don't just "read" this book. Pass it along to a friend. Order additional copies to distribute to everyone you meet. Use it to promote prayer for China and the suffering underground church. Use it to educate others about the need. Use it to send more Bibles to those trapped in the jaws of the Dragon. This is a book we have needed for years. I pray that God will bless it for His glory.

Pastor Dennis Balcombe
Revival Christian Church
Hong Kong, S.A.R., China
September 1997

Chapter I

Chen-Ma: Tortured for Her Bible

My hands also will I lift unto thy commandments, which I have loved (Psalm 119:47-48).

CHEN-MA clutches a beautiful, new Chinese study Bible in what remains of her scared, claw-like hands. Grateful tears fall as her mind rushes back to those terrifying moments when she last held a Chinese Bible.

It was almost 25 years ago, during the horror of Chairman Mao's Great Cultural Revolution. She has forgiven her Red Guard tormentors a thousand times since. But the day won't delete in her memory. She still blushes at the shame of public humiliation. She winces in pain recalling the Bible being crushed from her grip.

Chen-Ma's Bible was actually beaten from her broken fingers as she lay — stripped nearly naked — on the dusty streets of Taiyun.

Once, she had the strong, perfectly formed

fingers of a piano teacher. The remains of her hands ache as she recalls the cracking of bones — the sounds of torture meant to destroy her ability to ever again use her wrists.

The demon-possessed mob of Red Guards beat her hands with rods and pipes. Frenzied, they stomped on her fingers until they were not just useless — but almost unrecognizable. They wanted more than humiliation and pain. They wanted to make sure she could never hold a Bible again. Never play a piano.

In time, the flesh mended. Painfully. Slowly. But denied medical care by Communist hard-liners, the bones had to fuse without reconstructive surgery. There was no series of operations or rehabilitation to restore normal use. Today the remains of her hands extend from Chen-Ma's arms as paw-like appendages, her fingers frozen into claws.

In 1996 Chen-Ma chuckled with delight to discover she could still use those broken "hands" to read the words of Jesus. That was when an American Bible courier was finally able to replace her lost Bible — the book for which she had originally sacrificed her health. She uses the side of her hand to first bow a page; then hook it with a finger to make the turn.

But the tears which fell when she at last replaced her old Bible were tears of gratitude, not self-pity or regret. She would gladly do it all over again for the sake of her faith in Christ.

Sharing the Sufferings of Jesus Christ

In fact, Chen-Ma never complains. Even during the painful months when her hands "healed" without medical care she used her pain devotionally for God. Her injuries are a gateway to heaven for her, and have become her way "to partake in the sufferings of Christ" according to 2 Corinthians 1:7.

Chen-Ma, like many who live under anti-Christ controlled governments, comforts herself with the words of Peter and Paul for sufferers. The Bible has much to say to persecuted ones, much comfort for sufferers. That's one of the reasons the Red Dragon hates it so. "For the joy that was set before Him, Christ endured the cross — so what is this?" she asks, quoting Hebrews 12:2.

"We must learn to accept the trials and tragedies that come into our lives," says Chen-Ma, "and offer them as sacrifices to the Lord. As Christ accepted his death in Gethsemane — so must we offer our bodies and lives in obedience to the Heavenly Father." So today, Chen-Ma shoves her stumpy hands into simple tasks like turning the pages of her new Bible and sweeping the floor. She wields them as trophies of her love for the Lord — and for His Word.

My hands also will I lift up unto thy commandments, which I have loved; and I will meditate in thy statutes (Psalm 119:48).

A Living Martyr for Her Lord

Chen-Ma's story is not unique. It blends easily with millions of other persecution stories from the days of the Communist Revolution. All share the same theme. All tell of remarkable Chinese Christians who have learned to incorporate suffering into their faith.

Thousands of Chen-Mas in China today still suffer for the Bibles they love. And more are added daily under the new wave of persecution that began after the Tiananmen Square Massacre.

Of course, anti-Bible cruelty actually began long before the Communist Revolution and continues today for Chinese believers. But the Communist Revolution is especially important because it succeeded in creating the current famine for God's Word; a famine still felt throughout China. Scores of millions of Bibles were burned on Red Guard bonfires from 1964 to 1976.

By 1997, only 15 million Bibles had been replaced by the government-controlled Amity Press in Nanjing — leaving less than one Bible for every thousand Chinese believers.

Because the government will not print enough Bibles to replace those destroyed in the Communist Revolution, the only way for underground believers to get a Chinese Bible today is from couriers. These volunteers must carry them in by hand from Hong Kong, Taiwan or the free world — usually only 20-100 copies at a time!

The Dragon's War on Education and the Truth of the Gospel

Like so many of the living martyrs from the Communist Revolution, Chen-Ma was the daughter of much-respected Chinese parents. Her father was a leading pastor, scholar, and teacher who never opposed the Communists. Her mother was an accomplished pianist and teacher. Both were university graduates and therefore scorned by the Red Guards as intellectuals — a charge still being made against Chinese Christians today.

Chairman Mao referred to "intellectuals" as "hairs on the skin of capitalism." He promised that the Communist Revolution would destroy the skin and the "hairs would die."

Chen-Ma, their only child, also became a music teacher. Like her mother, she taught at one of the many Christian schools that were confiscated from Chinese believers when the Communist Revolution swept through Shanxi. After their school was secularized, Chen-Ma and her mother continued to teach piano students at the school and in their home studio. Many children of Communist party officials were among their students. At first it seemed like life would continue as usual.

Chen-Ma and Her Father

Chen-Ma's father was a patriot. He accepted the Communist Revolution — but viewed the struggle for political power as outside his job description and calling. He believed in the command of Christ to "render therefore unto Caesar the things which are Caesar's and unto God the things which are God's (Luke 20:25).

Not understanding the Red Dragon — the supernatural evil power behind the Communist Revolution — he tried to remain a law-abiding citizen and get on with his work. As pastor, he saw his first duty as caring for the spiritual needs of his congregation. He accepted the military victory of the Communists, and their right to rule in the secular realm. So as one leadership post after another was filled with Communist Party cadre, he soon found they wanted much more than mere compliance. They wanted control of the Church as well as the State. They saw the Church as a political entity, not a spiritual fellowship.

The Dragon Reaches Out for the Church

Still, he led his family and the flock in trying to cooperate with the new government.

The Communist idea of organizing church groups into something called "The Three-Self Patriotic Movement" sounded innocent at first. Many nationally known religious leaders joined Zhou En Lai in organizing it. On the surface, its main purpose seemed to be separating the Church in China from foreign control. So when the Communists demanded he join, he did so with the prayer that somehow it would satisfy the Dragon. Most of the other clergy in Shanxi did the same.

Besides, he could see it was futile to resist.

Those pastors who refused to sign the "loyalty oath" of the Three-Self movement were branded as "counter-revolutionaries." Their prison sentences were automatically 15 to 20 years at hard labor.

Yet soon after joining, he realized that his political compromise gained nothing for the Christian believers. The party leadership was not going to let him pastor his flock. The Three-Self Patriotic Movement was merely another step down to the Dragon's dungeon.

Lost in the Labor Camps of the Bamboo Gulag

In 1957, only a year after he joined the TSPM, he was ordered to report to a "re-education camp" along with most of the other local Christian leaders. There, he learned for the first time that he was a pastor of a "redundant" congregation! The pastors were all given paper and pencil. For weeks they were forced to write biographical confessions of real and imagined sins. Soon it became easy to admit to lies. Finally, he was forced to sign the ultimate Marxist confession of guilt — that caring for the souls of Christians was "unproductive labor."

For this crime against "the people" Chen-Ma watched her father paraded through the streets in a dunce cap. He was sentenced by a "People's Court" to "re-education through labor" in the "laogai" (Bamboo Gulag) forced labor camps. The family wept for him — and for themselves as well. Chen-Ma and her mother were branded with his "shame" in the community.

They didn't know it then — but he would never return to his family . . . his home . . . or his ministry. Like millions of others since, he disappeared into the death camps of the revolution. During the last 50 years, more Christians have died for their faith in China than all other nations on earth combined. Today, more people remain in prison for their faith in China than any country on earth. Over 1,100 laogai concentration camps house 170 million slave laborers.

The Chinese House Church Emerges

At first, Chen-Ma and her mother attended the new consolidated "Three-Self Church" for Taiyun. Their congregation was forced to merge with others into one ecumenical church. Chapels and houses of worship were confiscated. Church buildings were turned into warehouses, police stations, or government offices.

Catechism, youth groups, Sunday schools, and evangelism were banned. Bibles, hymn books, and all Christian literature of any kind disappeared along with women's groups, men's groups, and the many Christian social services once operated by the Church. As Marx and Lenin predicted, the institutional church was dying.

Chen-Ma and most other Christians dropped out of the organized "church." It didn't seem authentic anymore — or even safe for that matter.

She threw herself into her music and teaching — avoiding discussion of her faith whenever possible. She didn't have to lie. She simply went "underground" and let everyone assume she had given up the "superstition of Christianity." But she didn't stop reading the Word of God or secretly praying.

Then something happened that almost blew her "cover." Some of her mother's friends began gathering in their houses to pray and study the Bible. The group grew. Soon, her mother found herself leading a regular meeting in their "living room" piano studio. Dozens of similar house meetings were beginning all over town. The Holy Spirit was doing something new. But it wasn't going unseen. The Communist Party assigns party members as "safety watchers" on every block.

One of their duties is to spot unusual movements of people. And they were making regular reports on the large numbers of people at the piano studio. Chen-Ma's mother didn't know it yet, but she was breaking the law. In the eyes of the Communist Party, this was not a home Bible study. No, indeed. She had opened what the Religious Affairs Bureau in Beijing called an illegal, unregistered, "House Church." And she was no longer a middle-aged school teacher but an "undesignated" pastor. The inevitable happened.

PSB (Communist KGB) Raids Begin

The first raid came with little warning. Chen-Ma was upstairs. She wasn't a part of the meeting, but she could hear that the singing had ended. Elder Zhang had began to preach. Then she saw them from her window. Uniformed city police were gathered in little groups at each end of the lane. Plainclothes detectives gathered near them.

Suddenly there was an explosion of shouts below. Men were pounding on both front and back doors at the same time. The attack was well planned. "Open up!" they screamed, banging loudly on the doors with their batons. This is the PSB! Open up!"

The PSB (Public Security Bureau) Police are the "thought police" of China. Mao modeled them after Stalin's KGB in the former USSR. They are the secret police who handle political and religious "crimes" against the Communist Party.

It sounded like the doors exploded off their hinges. The police were inside. There was a lot of noise. She could hear some of the women scream as the police began to beat Elder Zhang.

Later, she learned that this was standard procedure. Whoever was speaking when the raiders arrived was automatically beaten by several police. It was a warning to the others. The doors were blocked. The Christians were not allowed to leave the room. They were forced to watch as the preacher was bloodied. Others who appeared to be leading the meeting were also beaten — then dragged out to a waiting van. Bibles, books, and song sheets were confiscated.

That night, they also took down everyone's name and address. Then they took Elder Zhang and Chen-Ma's mother into the detention center for interrogation. They beat them again. In the morning they let them go without pressing any charges. This was only meant to be a warning.

Sometimes, police would beat leaders on the head, knees, elbows, and feet. This can cause crippling dislocations that take months to heal. Longer beatings — sometimes including water torture, electric shock, and rape — are often used.

The PSB raids on house churches are requested by the Religious Affairs Bureaus in Beijing and provincial capitals. They are designed to scare, terrorize, and intimidate "good" people — not catch violent criminals. The RAB uses them to force underground "house church" leaders to register — the first step toward closing down their meetings. The plan didn't work on Chen-Ma's mother.

Mother Sent to Prison

At school, Mother was reassigned from classroom teaching to janitorial work. She was held in "administrative detention" all night. Like Chen-Ma's father, she was asked to write her autobiography and "self-criticisms." In them, she had to confess her "class sins" against the revolution.

"Struggle sessions" were held for hours with Communist Party officials on the faculty. In these sessions, co-workers were encouraged to scream at her — yelling insults, slapping her face, and ridiculing faith in Christ.

Chen-Ma had avoided her mother's house meetings. Now she had to shun her mother as well.

This kept her from such struggle sessions and from prison.

Spies from the Three-Self movement must have convinced the party that Chen-Ma's mother was beyond "rehabilitation." After the next raid on the house church, she did not return. She was held in "judicial detention" without trial.

Detention time was needed for her tormentors to torture further confessions from her and work up a case. In 1961 she was sentenced to 20 years at hard labor. Chen-Ma never saw her mother again. Both her mother and father eventually died in labor camps.

"Blacklisted Daughter"

For the next five years, Chen-Ma lived almost peacefully and without incident. She avoided all worship services — both in the Three-Self movement and house churches. She continued to teach music and was popular with students. There was never a question about her professional qualifications. Other faculty at school treated her with cool but distant respect. She was a classic "old maid" school teacher.

However, Chen-Ma's parents were still well-remembered in the community. And because of that, she was a "black child." That meant she was named on the party's "black list" of potential enemies. Because of her family background, she was always passed over for promotions or commendations. That was fine with Chen-Ma. She had no ambitions except to be left alone with her Bible and piano. Her sole comfort was a deep but secret devotional life — and the precious Bible she read daily. Chen-Ma loved the Lord Jesus and that was all she needed. She continued daily prayers. She studied her beloved Bible morning and night. It was a habit begun when she was a child. Now, the Bible became her life jacket in a sea of chaos, turmoil, and despair. And she was about to need that life jacket more than ever.

The year was 1966. Chairman Mao, who claimed to be one of the only true disciples of Marx and Lenin left, was ready to begin a second generation of Communist rule. The youth of China were trained to treat him with god-like reverence. He decided to use this power to destroy Christ and the Bible once and for all. He canceled classes. Closed schools and universities. Named the students "Red Guards" and sent them on a book-burning rampage. This was the start of the Great Proletarian Communist Revolution. Millions died in the years of mayhem and vandalism that followed.

The Maoists announced that they would destroy "The Four Olds": old culture, old customs, old habits, and old ways of thinking. Belief in God was the oldest "way of thinking" — even older than China itself — and therefore it had to be destroyed.

The Communist "Red Book" of Atheism

The Red Guards had their own "anti-Christ

Bible" to guide them in selecting "old" victims to destroy. It was called *The Thoughts of Chairman Mao*. The little red book looked like a pocket New Testament. But instead of Christ's message of love and forgiveness, it taught Red Guards to covet, envy, hate, and seek violent vengeance on those Mao feared.

Maoist hard-liners studied "Mao Thought" in all training sessions, much like Christians studied the Bible. Afterwards, they went out into the streets to take "revolutionary action" against other Communists, small business owners, Christians, and anyone else who refused to bow to the Dragon (see Revelation 20:20).

Like all school teachers, Chen-Ma was ordered to suspend classes and help draw "big character" posters with the Red Guard students. In huge, bold Chinese letters the students were urged to identify people who represented "The Four Olds" in Taiyun.

No one, it seemed at first, was exempt. Using the little red book to guide them, they targeted authority figures for persecution. Parents, pastors, priests, and teachers were first on the list. Gradually the campaign reached out to entertainers, journalists, and government and Communist Party officials who were out of favor with Maoist hard-liners.

The Reign of Terror Begins

Chen-Ma was handicapped by her own family background, and soon her name began appearing on posters as "a puppy of the running dogs of superstition."

Beating drums and gongs, the Red Guard students paraded around the city for months. They usually plastered posters on church buildings, homes, offices, and temples of their victims first. This came days and sometimes weeks before an attack. The violence was premeditated. Calculated. Cruel. To take such "action" against respected older people, the Red Guards seemed to need some justification. That's why the posters began by making charges of crimes — using curses, obscenities, threats, and warnings.

Christians and Buddhists were especially targeted because Communists said their beliefs came from outside China — conveniently forgetting that their doctrines also came from Russian Communist missionaries.

One of the typically vulgar posters on Chen-Ma's house accused her of "Smelling foreign farts and calling them sweet."

Other posters accused her in vulgar street language of "Prostituting superstition, exorcism, and healing the sick." Chen-Ma laughed as she read them. If only the posters were true! Most of the time she was hiding her light under a bushel — not witnessing for her faith as she knew she should. She was certainly not delivering the possessed from demons or healing the sick.

"Help me today," she prayed one morning at dawn. "If they're going to accuse me of evangelism, help me to be a witness for you when my turn comes!"

Little did she know how God would answer her prayer before nightfall. The swelling volcano of hatred was going beyond words. She heard the marchers coming. Chen-Ma knew that the time had come for "revolutionary action" against her person. That always meant at least looting and vandalism — sometimes injury and death.

"Lord, will You give me the courage to speak for You? How can I witness in my hour of trial?" She remembered the Bible promise that the Holy Spirit would give words to witness when we are dragged before kings.

Communists Burn the Bibles

Chen-Ma heard the angry students chanting their hatred from blocks away. There was no escape now. She prayed for grace to face them. To show the same love Stephen and Jesus Christ had when they forgave their tormentors.

She still couldn't believe it. How could some of her own students — children she had taught and tutored — now be coming to loot her house?

What would she say? Would she be strong enough to show Christ's love? She met the teenagers calmly at the gate.

A youthful leader, bullhorn in hand, led several hundred students in chants against her:

"Criticize religion! Promote atheism!" he cried.

"Down with the imperialists!" replied the mob.

The chanting picked up cadence.

"Criticize religion!

"Down with the capitalist running dog!

"Promote atheism!

"Long live our Great Proletarian Cultural Revolution!

"Criticize religion!

"Long live our great leader Chairman Mao!

"Promote atheism!

"Down with superstition!

"Criticize religion! Promote atheism!"

Finally, the eyes of the Red Guards were filled with enough self-righteous anger and indignation that they could go on with the next step. "We are the Red Guards!" they announced triumphantly. "We have come to take revolutionary action against you. Stand aside!"

The Chaos Begins

Chen-Ma stepped politely aside and the "revolutionary" vandalism began. The youths went room to room. Apparently anything in print was suspect. They turned drawers and cabinets inside out.

Soon they appeared with armloads of books and sheet music. They stripped the walls of Christian art and her mother's framed scripture texts. Her father's library books were all added to the growing pile on the street. Tears came into her eyes. It was definitely a bonfire in the making — but so far they hadn't found her precious Bible and diaries.

She could hear the smashing of glass and furniture in the house. Then came the unmistakable sounds of piano strings vibrating. The Red Guards were dragging her piano across the floor and into the street.

"That is only a musical instrument," said Chen-Ma, careful not to show emotion as the piano appeared. "Has Chairman Mao asked you to destroy pianos too?"

Suddenly, a hand shot out to slap her face. More blows fell. She could taste the blood running down to her lips from her bleeding nose.

The leader motioned wordlessly for the piano to be added to the pile. Then Chen-Ma was forced to climb up barefooted on the piano stool and face the crowd while the chanting continued. Clods of mud and dog feces hit her face, mixing with her blood and tears.

A Spectacle for Christ

But before the bonfire could be lit, the Red Guards had to publicly "struggle" against her. This was part of the program. A poster was hung around her neck reading "Whore of the Imperialists" while various teenagers took turns accusing her of being a spy for the Americans and teaching the Bible.

Her arms were held painfully behind her back, forcing her to bow forward with her face to the ground as the youth verbally abused her.

Finally, the fire was lit and the teens took turns

feeding the flames with books and the sheet music of Brahms, Beethoven, Handel, and Mozart.

Chen-Ma saw her prayer diaries tossed onto the flames but her Bible was not with them. Then she saw it. The Red Guard leader dramatically held up the Bible. Just as he was about to throw it onto the flames, Chen-Ma jumped down.

"No!" she cried, snatching the Bible from his hands and clutching it to her chest. "Please let me keep this. You can burn everything else!"

Fury appeared in the eyes of the astonished leader.

Suddenly from behind, Chen-Ma felt two hands grab the yoke of her loose-fitting blouse. In one painful jerk, it was literally torn off her back.

She was dressed only in her baggy trousers now. She clutched the Bible against her small, naked breasts. Using her arms and the Bible, she tried to preserve her modesty as the crowd jeered in laughter.

Passing the Trial of Faith

"If you know what's good for you," threatened the leader, "you'll throw that book of superstition and lies onto the fire. Don't make me take it from you."

Chen-Ma instinctively knew that this was the test she had prayed to pass. The Red Guard leader could not back down. The mob and her neighbors stood in total silence, waiting to see how Chen-Ma would answer. Would she obey God or man?

Not to throw her Bible on the fire would be a terrible act of defiance — but a powerful way to witness to her first love.

Everyone would know that Jesus Christ was first if she refused to surrender the Bible now. The Red Guard leader had unwittingly given her a chance to witness to her neighbors and everyone. She spoke clearly but gently. She wanted even those hiding behind locked doors to hear — but not to seem arrogant.

"You can do whatever you want to me," she said with a courage that she knew could only come from the Holy Spirit. "This is the only book I need. You can burn all the rest."

The Red Guards hesitated. The leader tried to judge the mood of the crowd. He was clearly on the spot. Only the crackling sound of the burning piano could be heard.

A Whole Night to Deny the Faith

Murder was in his eyes as he spoke. "I'll give you the night to think about it," he shouted. "You'll stand here on your stool all night and think about it. Tomorrow, we'll be back to get your Jesus book."

Red Guards were posted with orders to keep her on the stool. So Chen-Ma stood all night, topless and barefoot, on the piano stool. She held the Bible firmly as darkness fell and the chill fall air turned numbing cold.

She fell asleep and crashed to the ground a

couple times but was forced back on the stool. She was not allowed to get down, even to go to the bathroom.

Christian neighbors must have prayed. In the morning she was filthy and tired — but still strong in spirit. She didn't even consider surrendering her precious Bible.

By 10 a.m. the mob returned again — only twice as large as before. Many carried bamboo sticks and the kind of iron bars used to reinforce concrete walls. They marched and chanted, repeating yesterday's whole performance again. They held another "struggle session" against her — cursing and ridiculing her faith in Christ. They mocked her love of classical music and her devotion to God's Word. She was denounced as a superstitious turd. Finally, the moment of truth came.

"Even though you don't deserve pity, we have tried to show revolutionary mercy and restraint," said the cadre, holding an iron bar menacingly before her eyes. "You have had time to surrender your old ideas and this old book of superstition. Give it up now and you can go inside and rest."

Chen-Ma remained silent.

Someone must have understood her silence for what it was.

Before the cadre could even reply, she was tackled from behind. Her whole body went flying forward off the stool. Somehow she managed to hold onto the Bible as she hit the ground.

A hundred hands grabbed her body. Her arms

were stretched out in front of her. As she was dragged forward across the ground, she could feel her trousers being pulled down. She realized she was now wearing only her underwear as the bamboo rods began flailing away at her legs and back. But she still held onto the Bible.

Then, while others held her forearms down, the leader began using the iron bar to deliberately beat her hands and wrists. The Bible slipped from her fingers. The pain in her hands replaced all feeling. Then the sky went black. Even after she lost consciousness — the blows did not stop.

When she awoke from the cold, she was in the house alone. It was night again. She was covered with blankets but still freezing. There was no fire — but she couldn't even move her hands to start one. They were swollen, smashed, and broken. Even the slightest attempt at movement sent arrows of pain shooting to her brain. She held her hands as still as she could.

Her Bible was gone.

At first Chen-Ma thought she might die there. Yet the presence of the Lord was in the room — and she knew that she would live. Unconsciousness mixed with shock came again, the only pain-killer she would have.

Sometime in the night, "angels" dressed her wounds. Christian neighbors appeared in the shadows to care for her in the months she was held under house arrest.

Chapter II

Heavenly Man: Red Dragon's Nightmare

And ye shall know the truth, and the truth shall make you free (John 8:32).

WHEN Yun was just 16, his father became very ill. The doctor said there was no hope. That night, Yun's mother heard a very gentle voice in the night saying "Jesus loves you."

She vaguely remembered, as a little girl, hearing about Jesus. How he healed the sick and fed the poor. That was before the Communists destroyed all the Bibles, the village church, and took the pastor away to a labor camp. It had been years since she heard about Jesus and the Bible, but now the power of that simple truth came back to her — Jesus loves me!

The very thought of that love was enough to force her out of bed and onto her knees. She prayed and repented of her sins. The forgiveness and love of the Lord was so real. Since Jesus really loved her, she decided to ask God for her husband's healing. She believed. Quite miraculously, the very next day her sick husband was healed. She began praising God to everyone. Aware that it was the name of Jesus that healed his father, Yun made a teenage decision to believe in Jesus — and serve him for the rest of his life. He asked his mother what he should do next. "Well, " she told him, "all the teachings of Jesus are recorded in the Bible — although I have never seen one."

From that day on, Yun longed to see a Bible. He asked other believers in their farming hamlet what a Bible looked like — but not one of them had ever seen one either. They did know of a former preacher who lived 30 miles away. Although the Communists had shut down the church he pastored, perhaps the old man could show him a Bible.

Ask for the Book of Heaven

Yun told the former pastor the purpose of his visit, but the old pastor was terrified. Seeing that Yun was so young and innocent, the old man would not dare admit that he had a Bible — let alone show him the hidden book.

"The Bible is the Word of God," he finally admitted. "It is the book of heaven. No man can buy a Bible in China today. But if you really want one, ask God for it. Fast and pray."

Yun had never heard of fasting, so the old preacher explained how to abstain from food. "When the fullness of time is come, the Lord will give you a Bible!" he promised.

Yun went home and fasted and prayed for two months as best he knew how. He prayed the same prayer over and over, "Lord, give me a Bible. Amen." When nothing happened, he went to the old preacher again, and explained his methods of piety.

"When you ask the Lord for a Bible," said the old man, "you have to weep before the Lord as well. The more earnest you are, the sooner you'll get your Bible. You just can't repeat words over and over to God. The Lord does not hear vain repetition."

So this time he ate only one meal a day, weeping and kneeling before God as he asked for a Bible. Several months passed. One morning, while sleeping, an old man appeared in a dream to him. "Brother Yun," he asked, "do you have anything to eat?"

"No," answered Yun. Then the old man handed him a steamed bun. As he stretched out his hand to receive it, the bread became a Bible in his hand! Then Yun awoke, weeping and telling the family that God had given him a Chinese Bible.

Mysterious Couriers Deliver a Bible

His parents believed that the fasting had driven him mad. He told them the details of his vision about the bun, and they were more convinced than ever that he had gone insane.

They were practical, hard-working farmers. Like all Chinese peasants, they were proud of being sensible and skeptical. "You can't fool us," they often boasted, "we weren't born yesterday you know." So Yun's new behavior and spiritual fervor made them fearful. Was Yun becoming a religious fanatic?

"If God has given you a Bible," challenged his father sternly, "show it to us. Where is your invisible Bible?"

At that very moment, two couriers walked into the room through the open farmhouse doorway. Both were dressed as travelers. They were obviously not from any nearby hamlet. No one recognized them — nor did they seem to greet or recognize anyone in particular.

"Holy Spirit has sent us to answer your prayer," said the taller man.

Yun's father did not tell them of Yun's prayer. But he politely asked if they had eaten, offering them tea and seats on one of the round steel stools the family used.

"No thank you," said one of the men, "we cannot stay to fellowship or take any food. We have come only to bring you a Bible."

Then reaching into his shoulder bag, he pulled out a book wrapped in newspaper and rubber bands. Ignoring the head of the house and the elder children, he handed the book directly to Yun.

"Holy Spirit told us to deliver a Bible to this house," said the tall man. Without any other explanation, they left the room. Neither of the Bible couriers were ever seen again.

With this second miracle, the family began to believe more surely than ever in the living God of the Bible — and in the Lord Jesus Christ whom Yun had vowed to serve.

From that day forward, Yun began trying to memorize one chapter of the Bible each day. He was soon able to visualize many pages of the Gospels. He could see the Chinese characters clearly in his mind — and easily recalled whole sections of God's word. He wanted to hide God's Word in his heart so that he would never, ever be without the Bible again.

The Bible was becoming the bread of his life — just as the vision predicted. Like the manna which the children of Israel ate in the wilderness, the Word of God became his daily food.

There was no pastor, church, or congregation in his village to guide him in his Bible study. However, Brother Yun was using every spare moment to absorb the Word of God. He was especially attracted to the Book of Acts and the missionary travels of Paul the Apostle.

Called to a "One Book" Itinerant Ministry

One day as he was reading the Book of Acts in 1984, the Lord appeared to him again in a vision. God reminded him of the teenage vow he made when he accepted Christ. Three times in the vision He told Yun to take his Bible and go preach the Gospel. He even told him where — to Henan and Hebei Provinces.

This was the beginning of Yun's missionary travels in rural South Central China. For the next several years, his illegal "Bible journeys" brought the Word of God to tens of thousands of people. As a result, thousands of new house churches sprang up. Everywhere he went, families turned to God as he shared the story of the Bible.

Brother Yun had become a "one book man." Except for the Bible, he had no other source of Christian instruction. He had never met or seen another evangelist or itinerant preacher/teacher. He had never been to high school or college, let alone a Bible school or seminary.

In fact, when he started his Bible ministry, he didn't even know that the government-controlled Three-Self Patriotic Movement had established "seminaries" to indoctrinate and train Christian clergy.

He had never heard a Christian radio program, read a Christian book, or attended a Bible camp or conference! All he had was the Bible in his mother tongue — and that was all he needed.

As a result, Yun's only pattern for ministry was the apostolic examples of Paul and the Apostles as recorded in Scripture. His only understanding of church/state relations was what he read about in the Gospels and the Book of Acts.

Just as the Bible taught, he expected hostility from the powers of this world — but he did not invite trouble or rebel against the government. He believed that God had created marriage, family, and government as good — but that sin had marred them. Only Christ could redeem us and our fallen world from sin. This was the message of the Chinese Bible, and like Paul, Brother Yun could only say "Woe unto me if I preach not the Gospel" (1 Corinthians 9:16).

So, he set out — dressed as the simple farm boy he was — walking from village to village with his Bible. He had no trouble blending in with the villagers because he was one of them. Brother Yun was a native missionary in every sense of the word.

He knew the fear and hatred the Communists carried in their hearts against Christ and the Bible. So he avoided larger towns with police stations and strong Communist Party organizations. He seldom stayed longer than a night or two in any place. In this way, he was gone before the authorities could arrest him.

Every night, he preached and prayed with tears steaming down his face. Healings and miracles happened effortlessly and naturally as Brother Yun shared the Word. Yun simply imitated the Bible stories and lives of the Apostles. The Book of Acts was normative to him.

"If God healed through Peter," he reasoned, "then why not through me? If the disciples and Paul cast out devils, why not his disciples today?"

Brother Yun simply lived out the life he had absorbed from his Bible reading! He took God's Word at face value — never mixing it with the doctrines of men and his own interpretations.

Explosive Growth of Christianity Brings Intense Persecution

Many "Closet Christians" who had been hiding since before the Communist Revolution came out and revealed themselves when Brother Yun appeared. They would often invite Brother Yun to stay in their homes. He taught by the light of single oil lamps until 1:30 or even 2:00 a.m. almost every night.

During the day, volunteers would slowly copy verses and passages by hand from his Bible. Many believers had been without a Bible or Bible teaching for 32-35 years — and they were starved for the lessons he shared. In most areas, Brother Yun's Bible was the first copy young people had ever seen!

He was especially concerned for these Bibleless youth. He began always traveling with young co-workers, just as Jesus commanded his original disciples. These "preacher boys" were trained by his example to memorize the Bible, plant New Testament churches, and minister the Word of God to the problems of the people. Brother Yun would often send these young people by train to gather Bibles from underground house churches on coastal cities. Thousands of these Bibles were being smuggled in from Hong Kong.

Each new Bible helped fan the fuels of revival. Without any promotion or publicity except the whispered invitations of peasants, tens of thousands attended Brother Yun's house meetings.

Churches were forming and revivals broke out almost everywhere Brother Yun went with his Bible.

Denied access to government church buildings, Christian literature, mass media, Sunday schools, and the humanitarian outreach they once offered their neighbors — the few surviving Christians now had only one thing to offer their neighbors. Brother Yun preached that Gospel from the only textbook he had — a single copy of the banned Chinese Bible.

After his first few weeks, he was secretly networking from one group of house believers to the next — witnessing along the way to their trusted family and friends. As Yun witnessed "one-on-one" with unbelievers, many were secretly baptized beneath highway bridges and in fish ponds.

Holy Communion services, which had stopped when church buildings were confiscated, began again in "living room" meetings. Almost every "preaching stop" on his Bible Tour produced one or two new "households of faith." Sometimes a half-dozen new house churches started up in a single week!

At first the eyes of the authorities seemed blinded to the presence of this fast-traveling, Bible-carrying evangelist. Among the peasants, he swum like a fish in seaweed. In fact, they didn't know if there was one or many "Bible Men" on the road. However, spies in his own village soon reported his activities. The police began looking for him. It was soon no longer safe to return home. His family and village were soon under regular surveillance by PSB agents and informers.

His family was shunned by neighbors and relatives — the worst shame any Chinese person can experience. It was dangerous to be friends with relatives of anyone wanted by the police. Yun rarely saw his wife or relatives, and then only in elaborately planned rendezvous-style meetings. In fact, by the time his wife Lingling delivered their first baby, he was already in labor reform camp.

Guided by the Holy Spirit, he was able to evade authorities and situations where he would attract public attention for several years. The result was the first underground house church " Bible Revival" in South Central China.

Betrayal in Heping

However, Public Security Bureau secret agents almost caught up with him in Heping. He was invited by local believers there to minister in a big house church revival. However, early in the morning on the day he arrived, the dreaded PSB raided the home of Pastor Enshen — one of the leaders. (He was eventually tortured and sentenced to labor reform camp where he became a government slave.)

As always, Yun waited till dark to knock on the door of his underground Christian contacts. Pulling him inside, his terrified hosts told him the news of Pastor Enshen's arrest. All house meetings had been canceled for the night.

What's more, they said the PSB had his name and knew he was coming. They had stopped by earlier looking for "Brother Yun." The frightened Christian couple was afraid to hide him for the night and warned him to keep moving.

"Get out of the town as fast as you can and avoid the People's Militia," they whispered. "The Communist Party cadre have called up a PM posse to search for you!"

Obviously betrayed for the first time, Brother Yun made his way carefully to the edge of town, moving with crowds. They spotted a militia road-block ahead checking identity cards. With his co-worker, Brother Ming, he hid on the embankment of a fishpond. They decided to hide all night in the open fields. Teeth chattering in the bitter cold, they sang softly in Chinese:

> In times of need, be joyous
>   — Love the Lord.
> In times of hunger, be joyous
>   — Love the Lord.
> In times of life or death —
>   Only love the Lord.

While it was still dark, around 4:00 a.m., Brother Yun saw a vision of great persecution coming to all of Habing County. He saw many believers being beaten, chained, and thrown into prison.

"Brother Ming," said Yun, "the Lord is showing me that we must leave Habing quickly." So

not even waiting for morning light, they escaped
— walking backroads to the train junction. They
had invitations from believers far to the north
in County A, and hoped to escape to them by
rail. God again blinded the eyes of authorities,
and they were able to catch a train without being spotted.

The Dragon Rages

In County A, the situation was also very tense,
but the believers eagerly welcomed Brothers Yun
and Ming. They risked death and imprisonment to
hide the two Bible men. There was no doubt that
the Dragon was awake now. He was ordering his
Communist Party pawns into action against the
Bible.

The anti-Bible hate campaign was obviously
becoming a regional program. Everywhere they
looked there were big character posters attacking
the "counter-revolutionary Christians" and ridiculing belief in God. Ming and Yun took turns preaching in all-night prayer meetings, encouraging the
believers to stand steadfast in adversity.

Yun and Ming learned that spies from the
Three-Self Patriotic Church had infiltrated their
meetings before Habing, pretending to be Christians. It was these false brethren who had betrayed
the Habing believers to a sadistic gang of government agents from the Religious Affairs Bureau
(RAB). Just as Brother Yun had been shown in his
vision, thousands were being "rounded up" for tor-

ture and slave-labor by the secret police in Habing.

Understanding that the hate-campaign was coming from the RAB national headquarters in Beijing, Ming and Yun began preaching from Acts 20:22-24. They wanted to prepare the believers for this new wave of torture and prison. Every few years, the RAB starts a new anti-Bible campaign, and the older believers realized that that another one was now starting up.

"To be a martyr for the Lord," sang Yun in every meeting, *"to be a martyr for the Lord, I am willing to die gloriously for the Lord."*

After a midnight prayer meeting in County C, Brother Yun and several others were leaving to get some rest for the night. As they walked to the home of a nearby believer, a gang of ten thugs ran out of the darkness shouting, "Stop! What are you doing there?"

The others with him turned and ran to escape. But Brother Yun was caught by the arm and quickly jabbed in the back with an electric cattle prod. The stun charge must have been set to maximum. The pain felt like a thousand arrows pierced his heart. The high voltage instantly knocked him off his feet and into a snow bank.

"Where are you from? What is your name?" shouted the men. "Answer quickly or we'll beat you to death right here!"

The questions came like a machine gun.

"How many are their in your gang?

"What are you doing here?

"How many are with you?"

Brother Yun felt a flood of peace flood his whole being as Scripture verses came to his mind. The Lord reassured him in his spirit with the word he had memorized. As the police thugs bound his arms painfully behind his back, he struggled to find a way to answer without betraying the others. The Lord brought to mind David and how he feigned insanity when captured by his enemies.

Loudly he shouted out for the whole neighborhood to hear, "I am . . . heavenly man . . . live in Gospel village. My name is New Creation. My father is . . . full of grace. My mother is faith . . . hope . . . love."

"What kind of nonsense is that?" yelled the sergeant, slapping his face. The other police began to follow his lead, kicking him. Then they used fists, feet, cattle prods, stun guns, truncheons, and gun handles to beat him.

They kept hitting him shamelessly as a crowd gathered. Many of the believers among the bystanders began to weep softly as the blood flowed from Brother Yun's head and face. This pleased the PSB police who continued to beat the innocent prisoner as the crowd grew. The cruelty was exactly what they wanted the whole neighborhood to witness.

A "heavenly man" — a "Bible man" from out of town was being beaten bloody. No one said a word or dared intervene. This would teach the people a lesson they would never forget.

Why Terror Tactics Against the Bible?

They might have killed him that night, but God protected Brother Yun. The PSB wanted to make an example of him. To terrify the whole community, not just the Christians. They hoped to frighten the weak-minded. To scare away as many as possible from reading the Bible and worshiping God in the house meetings.

The Dragon knows that terror works well on most Chinese people — so he uses it often and with murderous results. Over 30 million have been killed since the Communist revolution came to China from the old USSR. It was Lenin and Stalin who taught the Chinese PSB how to use terror against the Christians.

Terror is still widely used in China today. During the countdown to the 1997 takeover of Hong Kong, Communist agents started whisper campaigns in Hong Kong churches. They told true stories of pastors in China whose fingers were being broken with pliers by police torturers — and of others who were having holes drilled in their flesh with power tools.

They also threatened to execute several well-known pastors in China who had been arrested in the months before the Hong Kong takeover.

Why spread such reports of atrocities and threats among the Chinese people? Why leak such news to the Christian media in the west? Why risk world condemnation at a time when they wanted to look reasonable and humane?

Partly of course, the Communists release such propaganda because they know that the U.N. is powerless to stop them. And the United States is more interested in promoting trade than protecting human rights. So, figure the Communists, if the world doesn't care how Chinese police treat minorities and Christian prisoners anyway — why not brag about it?

But the real reason China is willing to risk world condemnation is simply because they know that terror works. Most people in Chinese society, and even many in the Christian churches, are easily controlled and intimidated by torture stories.

Deng Xiaoping, the Communist leader who ordered the Tiananmen Square Massacre, explained it when he said, "If you want to scare the chickens, kill a monkey." Bible believers in China have become the sacrificial monkey being killed to terrorize the chickens. So have many other non-Christian prisoners of conscience including Buddhists and Muslims.

Heavenly Man Begins His Ordeal

So Brother Yun's torment began. The PSB didn't know who they had yet — but they were sure he was from out of town. The police figured "Heavenly Man" had to be one of the traveling "Bible teachers" who were spreading the Word of God and stirring up the house churches.

No charges are needed for Chinese police to hold anyone for interrogation. They decided to detain "Heavenly Man" on the hunch that they had a criminal. At the police substation lock-up, Brother Yun was thrown into a cell with Brother Jian and three other brethren — all arrested leaving the same meeting where he had preached. They had been arrested at other checkpoints in streets and alleys surrounding the house church.

Brother Yun's shoes were taken away along with his Bible and shoulder bag. The cells were unheated and it was well below freezing outside. His whole body trembled and shook from the cold. He couldn't stop the shivers, which came over him in waves. The tight handcuffs and leg-irons made it worse. The more he shivered the more they cut into his aching, unwashed flesh.

Some old ladies from the house churches appeared at the station. They brought blankets, rice, and vegetables for the prisoners. Brother Yun overheard the jailer talking with the women.

"Do you have relatives here," he asked, "who is this aid for?"

"For the heavenly people," they replied.

Brother Yun praised God as the word "heaven" being used! His "Heavenly Man" witness in the street had already spread among the believers. Although the guards didn't share the mercy gifts with the prisoners, Brother Yun began felt warmer just knowing that believers on the outside were praying and loving them.

He began to praise God even when the blankets and food were not brought into them. He

turned over the still empty "toilet" bucket and
began to beat on it and sing. He remembered
Psalm 150 which says to use drums and cym-
bals to praise the Lord. The toilet bucket was
his "praise drum."

The guards were already wrapped in warm
quilts for the night — far too comfortable to get
up and stop the crazy "Heavenly Man" — so
Brother Yun and the others began their first night
in prison as Paul and Silas did. They thanked the
Lord for the privilege of suffering for Jesus' sake,
dancing and singing to the Lord.

Discovered by His Tormentors

In the months that followed, jail guards and
visiting PSB agents began taking turns torturing
Brother Yun. Each had their own goals. The guards
were determined to break his spirit. The PSB
wanted him to confess who he really was — and
disclose the names of other Bible believers.

But instead of crushing the heavenly people
— miracles, deliverance, and even ministry op-
portunities surrounded them in prison. Murderers,
rapists, and other political prisoners found Christ
and were baptized. Many believers were encouraged and renewed their walks with the Lord —
leaving prison as flaming witnesses for Christ.

Even when other prisoners were beaten to
death before his eyes, the Lord protected Brother
Yun and his companions. Although they were
starved and beaten often, supernatural protection

followed them from jail to prison and on to labor camp.

Then in January, the PSB chief from "B" City came to interrogate him. He immediately recognized him. "You put on a good act pretending to be insane," laughed the agent. "You think you're a clever man, but there is no way you can elude me."

Delighted to be rid of him, his jailers denied him food. Before transporting him to "B" City, the guards beat him up again. His eyes were blackened and his face was so swollen he was unrecognizable.

They crossed his hands and handcuffed them so tightly that his wrists began to bleed in the back of the open truck. Yun thought he would certainly die and asked the Lord to receive his spirit. But the Lord had other plans.

In the Jaws of the Dragon

His bloody clothing began to freeze on his body as a blizzard began. The truck drove on for hours. Even slight movements of the vehicle caused the handcuffs to cut deeper into his wrists. The Holy Spirit brought Scripture after Scripture to memory.

"Be still and know that I am God. . . . The Lord of hosts is with us; the God of Jacob is our strength," came to mind as the truck finally drove into the streets of "B" City.

Everywhere there were red and green banners "welcoming" him to the city:

CELEBRATE THE ARREST OF COUNTER-REVOLUTIONARY YUN BY THE PUBLIC SECURITY BUREAU!

THE APPREHENSION OF COUNTER-REVOLUTIONARY YUN IS GOOD NEWS FOR THE PEOPLE OF 'B' CITY!

BE RESOLUTE IN STRIKING DOWN THE CHRISTIAN COUNTER-REVOLUTIONARY LEADER YUN!

Brother Yun was shocked to see the banners everywhere around the gates of the PSB Detention Center. News of his arrest spread quickly across three provinces and many officials rushed to see him. A show trial of sorts was to start immediately.

What they saw was a short, skinny man covered with blood and half-starved to death. He weighed less than 100 pounds. Several of the officials could not help laughing out loud. Dressed in bare feet and rags, Brother Yun stood waiting for the judge to appear. He looked more like a clown than the dreadful counter-revolutionary of party propaganda.

One PSB cadre came up and spoke directly to Brother Yun, "We have a net covering the heavens that is without any holes. Even if you had three heads and six arms, don't ever think you can escape the long arm of our law!

"Today you had better admit defeat. Your co-workers have already fallen into our hands. Your church is now finished and you are totally defeated."

Brother Yun's Trial Begins

The judge was condescending and conciliatory when Brother Yun was arraigned that night. "Yun, you've gone through enough for today. You should realize by now how serious your crimes are. But the policy of the party is that of leniency towards those who confess, and severe punishment to those who resist.

"Today, the government is giving you a way out. All you have to do is to report honestly in detail about your activities during the past several years, exactly how you opposed the leadership of the party and the details of your organization. After which you will be set free and allowed to return to your home, family, and mother and be with them during the lunar New Year."

Yun was tired and confused but he remembered how Paul answered in his trials. "Look," he said, "I have been beaten in this manner and for several days have not eaten. I have no strength to speak. Moreover, what you want to know has been going on for many years. I cannot recall the details right off. I request that you give me several days to think about this. Then I will tell you about it."

"All right," replied the judge. "I will allow you time to consider. But how many days will you need?"

Yun answered, "The day that I have thought this through I will notify you."

So began one of the greatest struggles of his life. As each one of the four sets of prison gates closed behind him, he felt he was entering a den of devils. For the sake of the Gospel, he vowed not to eat or drink anything during the time of his trial and detention. He would fast and pray for spiritual strength to be completely victorious.

He had not eaten all day. The authorities wanted to show "the humanitarian face of the great revolution" so the guards brought him a stuffed dumpling and a bowl of celery pork soup. Yun was ravenous and Satan greatly tempted him to break his vow.

Yun gave his portion to the monitor of the cell who shared it with the other prisoners, who were all starving. They literally licked the bowl clean. This was an important beginning and one of the keys to victory for the 74-day miracle fast that he began that day.

Fasting for Victory

The judge offered Yun one more chance to confess voluntarily, but Yun again asked for more time and got it. After ten days of waiting, the impatient prosecutors decided to go back to interrogation and torture — but like the Lord Jesus standing before Pilate, Brother Yun was prepared. He decided he would not open his mouth before his accusers.

As he fasted and prayed, he was able to recall the very pages of God's word on the viewing screen of his mind. He saw the Chinese characters that represented the way Christ died, of Joseph in prison, of Daniel in the lion's den, of the three courageous young men in the fiery furnace.

He meditated on how Stephen was stoned to death, on how Paul reacted to his beatings and stonings, and how Peter was delivered from prison in Acts 12. He sang Psalms 23, 34, 146 and Romans 8:35-39.

As Yun was taken to the torture chamber each time, he quoted Psalm 119:11, "I have hidden Your word in my heart that I might not sin against You."

Too weak now from lack of food, the PSB agents had to ask another prisoner to carry him. He was so thin that his cellmate could carry him easily in his arms, just as if Yun were a child.

They asked him several questions, but he lay on the floor motionless. He did not even open his mouth. Thinking he was pretending, they started giving him cuts with their leather whips.

"Since the day this man entered prison," said his cellmate, "he said his head and chest were very painful — and he has not eaten anything in 10 days."

Realizing that he was too weak to talk, the PSB ordered him moved back to his cell.

Toward 40 Days and Beyond

They returned for him several times over the next weeks, using every method of bondage, threat, and torture they knew. Nothing could force Brother Yun to open his mouth or talk. He simply closed his eyes and read page after page of the Bible in his mind during torture sessions.

As his fast entered the 38th and 39th days, the Dragon appeared to Brother Yun and spoke to him. "Yun," said Satan, "Jesus fasted only 40 days. Can the student be greater than the teacher? How can the servant be greater than his Lord? How can you surpass 40 days?"

The Dragon's words were more awful than all the beatings and torture. Yun was overwhelmed by doubt, fear, and discouragement. The Dragon even suggested suicide — and Yun might have killed himself but for the fear of breaking Commandment VI.

Then the words of Revelation 3:8 appeared before his mind's eye in Chinese characters, "My son, I know your works: behold I have set before you an open door, and no man can shut it: for you have a little strength, *and have kept my word, and have not denied my name.*"

Brother Yun begin to sing the words of Psalm 146:2-10, " While I live I will praise the Lord: I will sing praises unto my God while I have my being. . . ."

Then it happened. The Word of God came

with an answer for the Dragon's temptation. Jesus
said, "Verily, verily, I say unto you, he that believes on me, the works that I do shall he do also;
and *greater works than these shall he do; because
I go unto my father*" (John 14:12). That was the
word Yun needed to go forward fasting for another 34 days!

On the 40th day of the fast, the judge called
him again to testify.

Before the judge, the PSB again used ropes,
whips, and stun guns to interrogate and torture Yun
but he continued to remain silent.

"We will beat you to death," they said. "You
were always saying that the government-approved
Three-Self Patriotic Church is harlot. Why is it that
now you are pretending to be deaf and dumb?"

Then the judge interrupted in a reasonable
voice, "Today we are giving you your last opportunity. If you promise to attend the Three-Self Patriotic Church, we will not only cease from investi-
gating your previous activities, but we will even
allow you to have the honorary, official position
of Chairman of the Church. Now you must tell us,
do you agree to this?"

Tears began to fall from Yun's eyes. He felt
such love for the poor judge, for the PSB sadists
who tortured him, and for all the ignorant authorities who did not know what they were doing. Their
temptation was so feeble, foolish, and transparent.
How could a child of God even answer such spiritual ignorance? He remained silent. There was no

reason to even try to reply to those whose eyes were so blind.

The court physician, a short, fat man dressed in white, then walked confidently over to Yun's side. He addressed the whole court. "So is it true that this man cannot speak? Look, I will get him to speak!"

Then he looked into Brother Yun's eyes with an evil, sadistic smile. "So you really can't speak? Okay, today I'm going to give you an injection to heal you of your mute condition!"

The doctor then ordered the guards to hold Yun down. From a box he took out six large needles, passing them before Yun's eyes to create terror. Then he grabbed Yun's hand and stuck the first needle under his left thumbnail. An intense pain shot through his whole body and Yun couldn't help but scream as the doctor twisted and turned the needle under his bleeding nail.

Then he did the same to his other fingers until, after the fourth needle was inserted, Yun fainted. When kicks and water thrown from the PSB men failed to revive Yun, the judge ordered him back to the cell.

"Take your stubborn mind and go meet your God!" said one of the agents as he threw Brother Yun back into the cell.

Life Today in Gospel Village

The rest of Yun's remarkable story is told in *Lilies Among Thorns*. How he was sentenced to labor camp, led hundreds of prisoners to Christ, and ministered even under house arrest to visitors from many counties, just as Paul ministered from Rome.

At his parole hearing, the head of the PSB gravely warned Brother Yun of his peril. "You should know that your problem is very serious. You should be severely punished. However, because your stubborn mind will not be changed even if we kill you, we have decided to allow you to return home under people's supervision. The following rules have been laid down by us and the local authorities:

> 1. You have been stripped of all your political rights and there is no way you can remove the hat of having been a political prisoner. You must come under the control and supervision of the local government. You are still a political prisoner.
>
> 2. You must report to the PSB once a month. The local authorities, cadres, people's militia, and all the people have the authority to supervise your activities. You cannot leave your village on your own. If any unknown person has contact with you, you must immediately be bound and taken to the police for investigation.
>
> 3. You must attend the Three-Self Church that is recognized and supported by the government.

Yun answered, "Respected leaders, since I have been stripped of all my political rights, how could I have the privilege of attending this great organization that is supported by the government? Is this not a contradiction in terms?"

The PSB chief was enraged by the reply, "Yun, you are so deceitful. We must sternly warn you that after you return home, if you dare to incite the believers to oppose the religious policy of the Party, you will bear the consequences!"

Brother Yun, his wife Lingling, and millions of other Bible believers in China are still living and ministering today under restrictions like these. No wonder they fear the words of Christ who said, "The Spirit of the Lord is upon me because he has anointed me to preach deliverance to the captives . . . to set at liberty them that are bruised" (Luke 4:18).

Chapter III

Brother Ralph: Getting Bibles Inside China Today

How beautiful upon the mountains are the feet of him that bringeth good tidings, that publisheth peace . . . that publisheth salvation: that saith unto Zion, Thy God reigneth! (Isaiah 52:7)

BROTHER RALPH finally retired from his plumbing business in Baton Rouge this year, so he's back in Hong Kong for his third Bible mission to China. This trip is not for just a week or two — but three whole months.

"Time is short," says Brother Ralph seriously, "and I never know which trip will be my last. I don't know when the Lord will return, when I will go home, or if Hong Kong security will close the doors to China."

For Brother Ralph, the new Hong Kong "Basic Law" of 1997 is creating an emergency that might go on for decades. The Beijing Communists have called on the churches of Hong Kong to adopt a new policy of "non-interference" with congregations in the rest of China. Many believe this could lead to new Bible shortages if distribution and printing Bibles from Hong Kong becomes harder.

Meanwhile, for thousands of Brother Ralphs, Hong Kong is still the gateway for Bibles to China. Each trip to Hong Kong costs him thousands of dollars — and time away from his wife and family in the USA. But Ralph is still convinced that Bible delivery work is the best investment he's ever made in the kingdom of God.

"We know that every Bible we bring into China results in an average of five Chinese being baptized into Christ," says Ralph as he lovingly holds up a copy of God's word in Chinese.

"Chinese Bibles win souls to Christ because God has promised that His Word will not return void. It will accomplish the purpose for which it was revealed. Every Bible that reaches a Chinese hand and heart is a missionary."

In Kowloon, Brother Ralph shares a tiny Fan Ling apartment with 12 other "Donkeys for Christ." Most nights, he sleeps on an upper bunk in a room with six other volunteers. The group is always changing. Couriers come and go from Australia, England, Germany, New Zealand, and all over the world. Every country, that is, except China. Chinese "donkeys" who try to cross the border with quantities of Bibles risk arrest, beatings, and jail — even if they have British or American passports.

Some Bible couriers come for just the thrill

and joy of one border crossing. Others stay a week or two, making 6-10 crossings. Every Bible courier group has some who have been carrying Bibles for six months, a year, or even longer. They're called "donkeys" because they hand carry Bibles to Chinese believers.

Almost every day — five or six times a week — Brother Ralph and his teammates load up their bags with 25 to 100 Chinese Bibles. Then, by boat, bus, or train they make the 50-mile border crossing to Guangzhou.

One Bible Shared by Whole Congregations

Ralph made his first China Bible journey with a Nora Lam Bible distribution team in 1988. It was during a brief period of openness that started the early heyday of economic reform. Chinese Christians were feeling confident about the future. They were not afraid to talk with foreigners, or members of the Nora Lam Bible distribution team.

The group visited both registered and unregistered congregations in Beijing, Guangdong, and Nanjing. Everywhere, Ralph saw evidence of the tremendous need for Bibles.

Even most registered church buildings were without pulpit and pew Bibles.

There was less than one Bible for every thousand Christians in China in 1988, and the situation is not much better today because revival is exploding in China!

The Bible is simply not available to the average Chinese citizen. The government was letting small shopkeepers open private stores then — but even in the capital city of Beijing, Ralph could not find a single book shop or stall that displayed Bibles!

Even in the black markets that illegally sold other banned books — pirated software, western newspapers, magazines, and pornography — it was and is impossible to buy a Bible.

Only One Legal Bible Press for All of China!

The Nora Lam team visited Nanjing where the group was welcomed to visit the tiny Amity Bible Press. It is still the only press in the country authorized to print Bibles for the government-controlled "Three-Self" congregations, which must also make a commitment to the teachings of communism in order to be authorized.

In 1997, Amity Press announced that they have printed only 15 million copies of the Bible so far. The Religious Affairs Bureau in Beijing unofficially admits that there are 97 million Christians in the motherland now.

"I'm no rocket scientist," jokes Ralph, "but when I saw that tiny Amity Press, I knew that they would never get the job done. Even if Amity Press prints Bibles around the clock on three shifts, it couldn't even print enough to keep up with the needs of one province — let alone all of China.

"That's when I decided I would use the rest of my life to help get Bibles into China."

Cracks in the Bamboo Curtain

Brother Ralph didn't just talk. He started looking for cracks in the Bamboo Curtain. On weekends, he started visiting Chinese ships in port. When there were no Chinese sailors to visit, he went to Chinese restaurants, businesses, and the university. He met many Chinese Communist "graduate students" at the university who came to study advanced technology to modernize the Red Army.

Everywhere he went, Brother Ralph started giving out free Chinese Bibles. He learned that overseas Chinese would eagerly accept a Bible in their own language — if they were alone or felt they were safe from Communist cadres and spies.

Through friendships with overseas Chinese, Brother Ralph found ways to send many Bibles back into China. He also led many Chinese scholars and visitors to put their faith in Christ.

He also became an advocate of Bible delivery ministries, collecting funds for the Nora Lam Bibles for China Crusade. He already belonged to a Christian businessmen's club. He got them to collect an annual offering for China Bibles. He also talked with his pastor and denomination.

He began raising money personally — not just to buy Bibles but to ship and deliver them! He soon found that he could buy a New Testament or Bible for $1.25 but it would take three or four times that much money to deliver it into the hands of a Chinese reader.

Fact: The biggest expense in Chinese Bible ministry is not printing but distribution.

Chinese Bibles: A Global Ministry

Pretty soon, Brother Ralph was networking with Christians in Los Angeles, California; Norfolk, Virginia — and even abroad in Auckland, New Zealand and Vancouver, British Columbia!

Chinese ships were landing in those ports every day and he began to enlist others to help him distribute Bibles to seamen and other Chinese visitors. He began to understand that getting Bibles into China had to be a global program.

"Every person going to China is a potential Bible courier, including returning Chinese," says Brother Ralph. "Without the help of the global Christian community, China will never get the numbers of Bibles needed for their 1.3 billion people.

"Since the Tiananmen Square massacre, outside Bibles have become even more important" adds Brother Ralph.

"The Chinese believers say it is harder and harder now to get Bibles in China. The present campaign against the Bible — called 'Strike Hard' in Chinese — is cracking down on the few people who dare to print or distribute Bibles in China.

"So outside Bibles, brought in by foreign and Chinese visitors are more vital than ever."

Ralph discovered that every Chinatown in the world, from Bangkok to New York, seems to be linked directly into the heart of China. Through clans, business, and church connections, Chinese can carry Bibles to the motherland. Every Chinese Christian visitor from Taiwan to Nairobi is able to safely take at least a Bible or two home in their luggage.

Foreign businessmen and women, diplomats, and tourists can all take in a few small Bibles as well. In this way, hundreds of thousands of Bibles a year are getting through the Dragon's Bible blockade. Once in China, they are distributed through one-on-one contacts, friendships, and relatives.

Courier organizations have found that while some Bibles are being confiscated by border guards, hundreds of thousands are still getting through every year. Ralph's goal is to turn those thousands into millions.

Chinese Bible Smugglers Take Over

Once inside China, the real distribution miracles begin. "Donkeys for Christ" like Ralph and the other "go teams" often drop Bibles at "safe houses" set up in big cities to receive Scriptures.

In times when the PSB secret police relax persecution, it is sometimes possible to actually rent vans, trucks, or taxis to transport one or two thousand Bibles at a time!

These are delivered to registered and unregistered congregations. From there they are passed onto a nationwide network of Chinese Bible volunteers.

The Chinese Bible men and women are volunteer couriers. They exchange small parcels of Bibles in airports, bus depots, train stations, restaurants, and public parks. Eventually, the distribution chain ends as Bibles are transferred from believer to believer in coat pockets and handbags. Chinese Bibles are the world's most invisible books.

Nearly 50 years of Communist Bible and book burnings have taught the believers to always keep their Bibles hidden — even when at home or in church services.

Bible Distribution to Prisoners and New Believers

Of course, the churches are not the end of the line for Bible distribution in China. Getting Bibles into the hands of curious students in schools, the sick in hospitals, slave labor, and prisoners are the greatest challenges facing the Chinese churches.

From the fast-growing house churches, Scripture portions are getting into the hands of new believers — the ones who most urgently and desperately want to study the Word of God for China today.

Over 20,000 Chinese are coming to Christ every day — over 700,000 new converts a year — and many of them are in the "laogai" or Chinese "Bamboo Gulag." This network of 1,100 slave labor camps imprisons millions of Christians, who are active witnesses.

Many times, new believers have to make do with hand-copied portions of the Bible — or books of the Bible that have been reverently torn apart and shared among many prisoners.

Mother Sheng, a Bible woman, was captured by the secret police. Though tortured and raped by PSB thugs she remained a vibrant witness for Christ. She was assigned to a Red Army-owned garment factory that made clothing for export to the USA.

One day, a very young sister who had just come to believe in Christ came to her with tears in her eyes. "Mother Sheng," she said, "I truly thirst after God's word. Can you find some way to get me a Bible?"

Joyfully, Mother Sheng replied, "Daughter, put your heart at ease for God has provided."

She then gave her a notepad in which she had copied many Scripture portions. The new sister was so glad to receive these notes from the Bible that she began to dance.

Every afternoon, the prisoners were given one hour off from their sewing machines for free time. Two days later, the young sister came back to Mother Sheng and placed the notepad under her clothes.

"Mother I have memorized all the verses. I desperately need a Bible!"

Mother Sheng was able to get her a New Testament and she began to copy it at once. She had to do this most carefully under the eyes of the guards. After 10-14 hours a day of work, she hid under her blanket, letting a little light in since the lights were never turned off.

She would scribble furiously with all her might. But the long hours of labor left her body exhausted. As winter approached the thin blanket could not keep out the cold so she shivered as she worked. Her teeth chattered but she kept going in order to make copies of the New Testament for other prisoners.

Line after line of beautiful calligraphy, Scripture after Scripture, precious words flowed from her pen. She prepared one copy after another of the precious Bread of Life.

Often, she was tempted to sleep and she would find herself nodding off and her pen slipping from her fingers. But each time she would see a picture of the sisters with their hands outstretched, begging for a Bible. She would then wake up with a jolt and continue copying until the wee hours of the morning.

The completed hand copies were then given to other believers who skipped meals and rest periods to read them. Others would go to the bathroom in the middle of the night to read.

No wonder Brother Ralph and others are so dedicated to Bible distribution in China. There is a terrible shortage of Bibles and the crisis is growing worse. But there is something every Christian in the world can do to help China.

Chapter IV

Nora Lam: What Can We Do About China's Growing Bible Crisis?

For the Word of God is quick and powerful, and sharper than any two-edged sword (Hebrews 4:12).

My dear Christian Reader,

In this book I have tried to communicate to you the urgent crisis need for Chinese Bibles in China today.

The message of this book is simple: We are the answer to the Chinese Bible shortage. Our persecuted Christian brothers and sisters in Communist China need Bibles; and they are depending on us to get these Bibles to them. The newborn babes in Christ need the strength and power of God's Word to survive every day in the jaws of the dragon of communism.

My heart tells me you will help! The underground Chinese Christians are suffering increased persecution for their faith every day. In fact, there are more Christians in prison in Red China than any other nation in the entire world.

I understand persecution and oppression. I was born in China and suffered the atrocities of a forced Communist labor camp as a young woman. I was ready to die for my faith in Christ . . . but God miraculously spared me.

In 1958, I escaped from Red China. For the past quarter century, I have given my life to reaching my fellow countrymen and women in China with the salvation message of Jesus Christ.

Satan cannot rest and Satan cannot sleep while the wave of revival sweeps across China — with over 20,000 souls coming to Jesus every day. The evil Chinese government, whose heart is desperately wicked, has launched a war against God that they will not win; because God's people will arise across America in behalf of the suffering Chinese Christians and declare war on Red China's war against the cross of Christ.

Even as the Lord heard the cries of the Hebrew children in the bondage to the Egyptians, He has also heard the cry of China's persecuted Christians as the "The Dragon goes forth to make war with those which have the testimony of Jesus Christ" (Rev. 12:17).

As God promises, "I am the Lord, and I will bring you out of their bondage, and I will redeem you with a stretched out arm" (Exod. 6:5-6).

YOU AND I CAN BE A PART OF GOD'S

STRETCHED OUT ARM TO THE UNDER-
GROUND CHINESE CHRISTIANS BY SEND-
ING BIBLES TO CHINA!

Conditions in China are deteriorating rapidly.
I feel a desperate need for someone to help me
bring down this godless stronghold in China by
rushing the mighty sword of God's Word into the
heart of the Dragon (Heb. 4:12).

I don't believe that God led you to pick up
this book by accident. The desperately persecuted
Christians of China need our immediate help. This
is our hour to act.

I am asking every reader of this book to help
me launch a new phase of my China Bible Campaign. There are three ways to get involved.

First, everyone who reads this book can help
financially. For as little as only $5, we can distrib-
ute a Bible in China. Sometimes entire congregations share only one Bible. Pages are copied by
hand and distributed.

There is a Bible coupon on the last pages of
this book. Please tear it out and send it to my office today with your best gift, designated for
BIBLES FOR CHINA.

Second, please pass copies of this book
along to every Christian friend you know. I need
your help to educate people about how really
bad the Bible crisis is in China and what terrible persecution the Chinese Christians are suffering. Why not order a whole case of this book
from our office today — and give one out to

everyone who promises to read it?

Let's mobilize the whole Christian world to get involved in supplying Chinese Bibles. Make sure your pastor and local leaders get a copy so they can know the truth about China today. Let's get united as the body of Christ, to get as many Bibles into China as we can.

We must act now. As bad as the situation is in China, there are windows of opportunity to get Bibles in — and that's what our Nora Lam Chinese Ministries Bible Crusade is all about.

Please help me make your personal impact on the struggle for the souls of China. Remember, over 20,000 souls are coming to Christ every day in China. Why can't we supply at least 20,000 Bibles a day to China? Surely we can if we all work together. God bless you for your obedience to send the gospel into all the world!

> Your missionary to China,
> Nora Lam

P.S. Please return the Bible coupon near the end of this book. As my thank you gift to you for sending your most generous gift for Chinese Bibles, I will send a copy of the book *China: The Last Superpower* by my son Joseph Lam with Wm. Thomas Bray.

風雨中的救主

宋能爾佈道團 敬贈

Would you Respond to "China's Cry" for Bibles?

Together, we can arm underground Christians in China with their most powerful weapon– CHINESE LANGUAGE BIBLES!

The greatest need for underground Christians is Chinese Bibles!

CLIP HERE

For Those Who Love China – Join The Love China Club

"Remember them that are in bonds." (Hebrews 13:3)

You may sponsor an Underground Chinese Pastor/Missionary for $20 a month

God is leading people throughout America to stand in the gap for China's perishing souls. Nora Lam Chinese Ministries International has established the "Love China Club" for those who feel the burden of China missions.

- - - - - - - - - - - **CLIP HERE** - - - - - - - - - - -

MEMBERSHIP FORM – "LOVE CHINA CLUB"

☐ YES, NORA LAM, I want to be a Member of the "Love China Club" and help the persecuted underground Christians on a regular, monthly basis. I'm rushing you my first MONTHLY gift of:

- ☐ **$20 (assisting 1 Chinese UNDERGROUND missionary)**
- ☐ **$40 (assisting 2 Chinese UNDERGROUND missionaries)**
- ☐ **$60 (assisting 3 Chinese UNDERGROUND missionaries)**
- ☐ **$_____ (To help as manly as I can)**

Please send me the FREE ☐ **"Love China Club" PIN** ☐ **Monthly Breakthrough Letter**

NAME_____

ADDRESS_____

CITY_____ STATE_____ ZIP_____

Please make checks payable to **NORA LAM CHINESE MINISTRIES INTERNATIONAL**
Box 24466, San Jose, CA 95154. All gifts are tax-deductible to the fullest extent of the law.

FSOH7

Nora Lam Chinese Ministries
International
Mission
Statement

"Go ye into all the world."
Mark 16:15

Nora Lam Chinese Ministries International exists for the express purpose of communicating the Gospel of Jesus Christ throughout China, Asia and the world according to Mark 16:15 which says, "Go ye into all the world, and preach the Gospel to every creature." This mission is accomplished through evangelistic crusades, preaching, meetings, missionary tours, Bible distribution, humanitarian and relief outreaches, orphanages, missionary training, educational materials, television, film and any other media available to spread the message of Jesus Christ.

Bibles for China Program

"Heaven and earth shall pass away, but my Words shall not pass away." Luke 21:33

God's Word endures. Nora Lam Chinese Ministries International believes in the power of God's Word and has distributed over ONE MILLION BIBLES throughout China and Asia. Through our underground distribution network, we distribute Chinese Bibles throughout the countryside of China.